Two on a Bridge

The Workbook

A Companion Tool Designed to
Enhance Discussions Outlined in
the *Two on a Bridge* Guidebook

by

Linda L. Stampoulos

CCB Publishing
British Columbia, Canada

Two on a Bridge The Workbook:
A Companion Tool Designed to Enhance Discussions
Outlined in the *Two on a Bridge* Guidebook

Copyright ©2011 by Linda L. Stampoulos
ISBN-13 978-1-926918-90-7
First Edition

Library and Archives Canada Cataloguing in Publication
Stampoulos, Linda L., 1946-
Two on a bridge. The workbook : a companion tool designed to enhance discussions
outlined in the Two on a bridge guidebook / written by Linda L. Stampoulos.
Supplement to: Two on a bridge.
ISBN 978-1-926918-89-1 (bound).--ISBN 978-1-926918-90-7 (pbk.)
Also available in electronic format.
1. Self-actualization (Psychology)--Problems, exercises, etc.
2. Spiritual life--Problems, exercises, etc. I. Title.
BF637.S4S712 2011   158.1   C2011-906353-0

For all general information regarding other books, visit pompanobooks.com

Original cover art design by Jinger Heaston: www.jingraphix.org

Illustrated by David Miley

Extreme care has been taken to ensure that all information presented in this book is accurate and up to date at the time of publishing. Neither the author nor the publisher can be held responsible for any errors or omissions. Additionally, neither is any liability assumed for damages resulting from the use of the information contained herein.

All rights reserved. No part of this publication may be reproduced, stored in a retrieval system or transmitted in any form or by any means, electronic, mechanical, photocopying, recording or otherwise without the express written permission of the publisher. Printed in the United States of America, the United Kingdom and Australia.

Publisher: CCB Publishing
             British Columbia, Canada
             www.ccbpublishing.com

for Lynn

Other Books by Linda L. Stampoulos

Visiting the Grand Canyon, Views of Early Tourism

The Redemption of Black Elk

Black Elks Vermachtnis

Two on a Bridge
(Guidebook & Workbook)

Contents

Welcome to the Bridge 1

Part I: Getting Started 2

The Invitation 2

Session 1: The Power of the Place 5

The Challenge of the Troll 8

Session 2: The Powers of the Vision Hoop 10

Session 3: The Vision Hoop: The Power Over Demons 14

Session 4: The Vision Hoop: The Power From Your Center 18

Session 5: The Ghost Dance: The Power to Strengthen Belief 22

Session 6: The Ghost Dance: Power to Survive 26

Session 7: Stepping off the Bridge 29

Part II: Other Readings for Discussion 30

Black Elk's Vision 30

Name Your Heroes 31

Part III: Other Activities 32

About the Author 33

From the power of the circle to the mystery of the Ghost Dance, ancient healing powers are waiting for you to discover them.

This workbook is designed to serve as a journal for you to reflect on your thoughts and feelings as your journey progresses. As a companion tool for the Guidebook, this Workbook follows the steps you and your partner will need to take to achieve your goals. As is the Guidebook, it is divided into seven sessions. Each will review a source of power and offer a list of suggested readings for you to prepare for the next session with your partner. The workbook suggests activities you and your partner will complete during your time together. These activities are designed to help you access the different energy sources and hopefully make them a part of your life.

Part I
Getting Started

The first step on your journey is to provide yourself with a base, your own personal setting, an actual location from which you can begin. This place is just for you alone, without your partner. It will be here that you will find the quiet solitude to prepare for your next session with your partner and review the suggested readings and answer the accompanying questions.

Maintain your own special place, a base location just for you alone.

Your meditation here will begin with a certain state of mind, a level of awareness which will eventually lead itself to its own energy source.

The Invitation

Next, you need to select a partner, someone who will accompany you on your journey across the bridge. The individual you select is entirely your choice. However, prior to making your selection, review the workbook to learn the nature of the material. Your partner should be someone you feel comfortable with, someone you trust, and especially someone who is a good listener. Invite them to share some time, usually one meeting a week for about seven weeks. During this period, you will both explore the activities, the suggested readings, keep your own personal journal, and become familiar with the powers that surround us. The bridge becomes a platform for discussion as you make your way across.

Select and maintain a location for you and your partner to meet during your sessions.

The pages available for "Reflections" are very important to the success of your journey. As stated in the Guidebook, to get the most out of your sessions together, you must use the time in between meetings for reflection. As someone once wrote, "The time we spend together is worth the time alone." Soon you will begin to feel a rhythm in the process: coming and going from your special place will give time for reflection.

Use the Workbook as your journal to jot your thoughts while still fresh in your mind. These are usually the thoughts that come to you after you leave the session and are reviewing the conversation in your mind. I like to refer to them as "shadow thoughts," they are extremely important and unless you jot them in your journal, they'll most likely remain lost in the shadows.

Keep in mind, not everything covered in the Guidebook is processed in the Workbook. Read the appropriate sections in the Guidebook to prepare you for each session.

Session One

The Power of the Place

At your first meeting, discuss the following questions:

1. Do you feel that this place is the best place to meet? What was it about the place that especially stands out as a good place for discussion?

2. As important as the setting is, will meeting here distract you for your concentration?

3. Having decided on the place, are you beginning to feel more comfortable and open for discussion?

4. Are there any "ground rules" you'd both like to set? For example each partner should have equal time for expression.

5. Is there anything else you would like to share at this time?

Set the time _____ and date _____ for your next session.

It's Time for you to meet the Troll

The Challenge of the Troll

Perhaps one of the more engaging activities in this workbook involves a mythical troll who lives under and guards the bridge. He is mysterious, frightening, odd, but above all, demanding. He emerges from the shadows as you step on to the bridge and presents his challenge to both you and your partner. What he represents are those things in our lives which we would rather avoid and somehow get around.

The troll presents a challenge, a non-negotiable "must do" if you are in any way to successfully cross the bridge. You do, however, maintain some measure of control because his demand can be met by your naming of it. To be more exact, the troll's challenge is that you choose and name in the presence of your partner, one goal that you have been thinking about but have not yet acted upon.

Maybe it is a doctor's appointment or screening that you have been putting off; perhaps it is a phone call which is long overdue. Of even deeper significance, maybe it is making some clear change in your lifestyle that represents a healthier way of life. The goal can vary in terms of intensity but what can no longer vary is your actual addressing it and being proactive in its outcome.

Use some of the time during your "Reflections" to think about your goal to meet the challenge of the troll.

As your meetings progress, you and your partner will review your progress in satisfying the demand of the troll and assist each other in whatever ways possible. Remember, at the last meeting, the troll will again emerge from the shadows to exact his demand on both of you.

Reflections

Session Two
The Powers of the Vision Hoop

Preparation for Session Two

To prepare for the next few sessions, it would be helpful to read "The Vision Hoop: The Circle of Winters" found in Part II of the Guidebook.

Answer the following:

1. Explain how the colors making up the outside of the circle of the hoop tell of our life's journey.

2. Why is it often referred to as "The Vision Hoop?"

In the reading "The Thunder-Beings Speak," how does Joseph Campbell describe the importance of your having a special place?

What does he mean when he refers to it as a "bliss station?"

Session Two

1. Would you care to share your first Reflections with your partner?

2. Review your answers to the questions regarding the Vision Hoop and the Thunder-Beings Speak.

3. Are you ready to discuss your decision to meet the challenge of the Troll?

Set the time _____ and date _____ for your next session.

Reflections

Session Three
The Vision Hoop:
The Power Over Demons

Preparation for Session Three

To prepare for session three, read "The People on the Bus" and address the following:

1. Everyone has both positive and negative forces in their life; unfortunately there is never a perfect balance. How successful are you in keeping a balance of positive and negative forces?

2. Do you tend to deal with situations as they arise or do you often prefer to "handle" them later? Will you share an example?

3. Considering the shadow figures on your bus, can you name them and do they distract you? Is it similar to a Jack-in-the-box experience?

4. Do you really want the shadows to vanish or is there a part of you that wants them to keep traveling along with you?

5. If you were successful in getting a negative force "off your bus" how did it make you feel?

Read "Demon or Dragon?" and answer the session questions together.

Session Three

1. Would you care to share your Reflections with your partner?

2. Review your answers to the questions regarding The People on the Bus.

3. Having read "Demon or Dragon?" in Part II of the Guidebook, together answer the following questions:

   A. It's often difficult to determine if something is a demon or a dragon. How do these terms differ?

   B. What do you think Jung means when he suggests we can learn to slay our dragons?

   C. Some of us have more than our fair share of demons. How do you account for this?

   D. How important is it to determine real from imagined? Does it make a difference? How?

4. Have you both shared your decision to meet the challenge of the Troll?

   Set the time _____ and date _____ for your next session

Reflections

Session Four
The Vision Hoop:
The Power From Your Center

Preparation for Session Four

Now that you have had time to think about the positive and negative forces in your life, it's time to do something with them.

Next to the numbers below try and list at least five of each:

Positive forces

1.
2.
3.
4.
5.

Negative forces

6.
7.
8.
9.
10.

Session Four
The Power from your Center

Place the number of the positive and negative forces you listed in your Vision Hoop below. Remember to keep the negative forces as far away from the center as possible, close to the rim of your hoop. This process prevents them from gaining access to the energy of the center, the source of psychic power. The more positive the force, the closer it should be placed to your center.

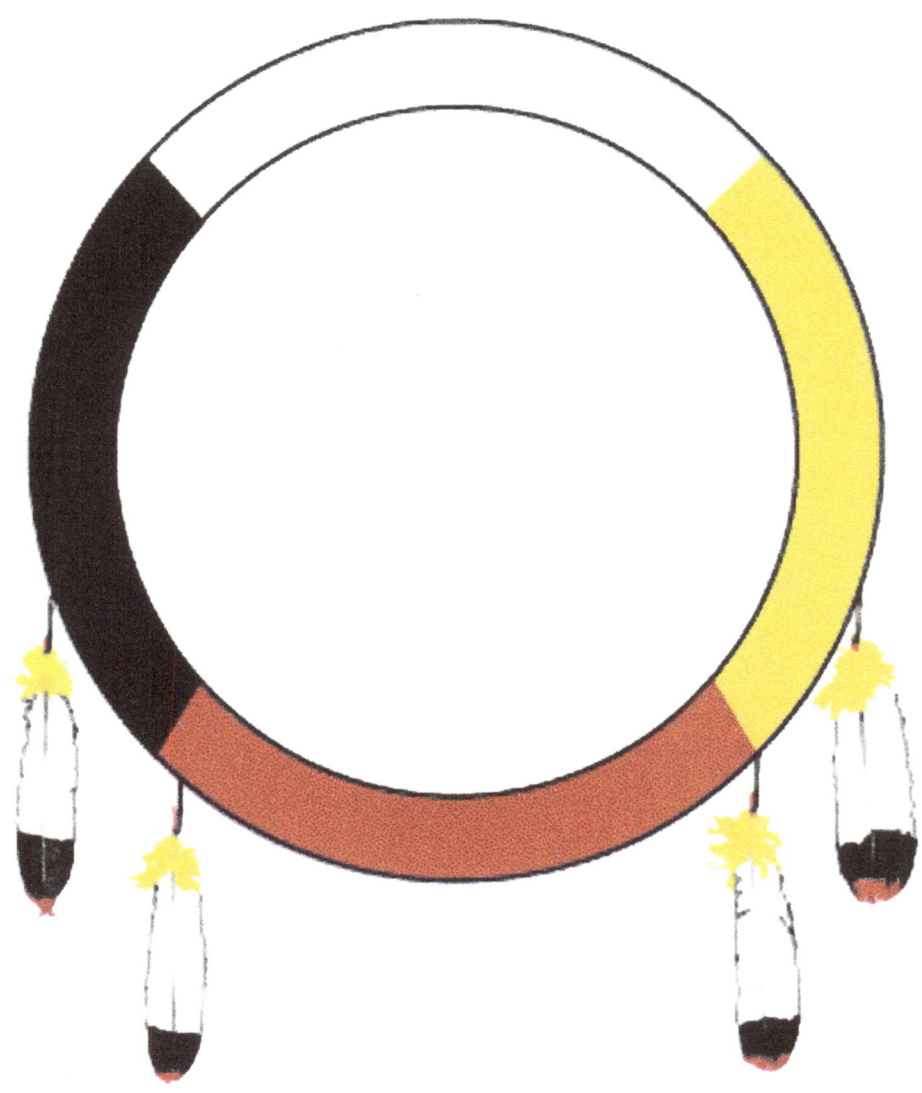

According to Campbell, when does the discovery

of your center happen?

Reflections

Session Five
The Ghost Dance: The Power to Strengthen Belief

Preparation for Session Five

Having read "But the Tigers Come at Night" in Part II of the Guidebook, together answer the following questions:

1. You probably recognize the title of this reading as a line from the song "I Dreamed a Dream" from Les Miserables. In the song the tigers came with their voices soft as thunder. The same can be said of the thoughts that enter our minds in the dark of night. Do you have a particular way of handling these "tigers?"

2. The essay tells of a particular style of mental gymnastics that offers a solution. Do you imagine that this is something that could be effective for you?

3. Thoughts that invade our sleep come with no invitation, and can be positive as well as negative. Are your "tigers" mostly negative or positive ones?

4. If you were to imagine a fantasy, is it one you would like to share with your partner?

5. If you have the opportunity, listen to the song and determine if the Tigers in "I Dreamed a Dream" are positive or negative.

Also for session five, read "The Ghost Dance" and become familiar with its purpose.

Session Five

The Power of the Ghost Dance

Would you care to share your Reflections with your partner?

Review your answers to the questions regarding "But the Tigers Come at Night."

The Guidebook lists a number of key principles and marked them as Guideposts. For session five, the following Guidepost was posted:

> The power doesn't necessarily come from those who have died, rather it comes from the belief in the power of the connection.

Although the Ghost Dance actually intended to bring back the dead, we can bring back their memory to provide comfort and strength.

How strong are you feelings of connection to those who have passed on?

Do you turn to the power of this connection during times of trouble?

Can you give one example of how a situation was helped by the power coming from the belief in those who have passed?

The Guidebook references the psychic connection as being a communication that comes through the senses. It leaves you with a feeling of a connection, a yielding acknowledgment of something that has gone before and yet continues to present itself as a dominant force. Have you ever experienced a psychic connection?

Reflections

Session Six

The Ghost Dance:

Power To Survive

Preparation for Session Six

Having read "The Bloody Snow" in Part II of the Guidebook, address the following:

1. Three days after the Battle at Wounded Knee, four babies were found alive under the snow, wrapped in shawls and lying beside their dead mothers. They had lived three days through a Dakota blizzard, without food, shelter, or attention to their wounds. What explanation can you offer that would best describe the "tenacity of life" so characteristic of indigenous people?"

2. Miracles happen everyday. Can you give an example of a miracle that affected your life?

3. The horrible event that happened at Wounded Knee marked the beginning of the end of the Ghost Dance Movement. The hope that came from bringing back the old ways and calling up the dead was left on the frozen, bloody snow. Yet something is rising from time, a new hope and a new day. Give your thoughts.

Session Six

The Ghost Dance: Power to Survive

Would you care to share your Reflections with your partner?

Review your answers to the questions regarding "The Bloody Snow"

In addition to miracles, we sometimes experience unexplained events, strange coincidences, and déjà vu occurrences. Often they happen without our realizing it, but later on, as we review the event, the strangeness rises. Can you share such happenings?

Being the next to last session it is time to visit the challenge of the troll. Have you accomplished this?

Session Seven
Stepping off the Bridge

Congratulations!

You have completed your journey and are about to step off the bridge. Hopefully you have a better understanding of the ancient powers that surround us. Through guided discussion you and your partner explored some of the problematic issues in your lives and with the help of the activities in this Workbook, you both are now able to take advantage of the "hidden hands" that are here to help you. By spending time in your special place, you will continue to recognize your own depths and gain that deep sense of inner peace and understanding.

You have the guideposts. You have the promise of the vision hoop. And, for a time, you had the comfort that comes from sharing time with a friend. Above all, you have the advantage of knowing the ancient energies that surround us, and most important, you have the nourishment that comes from the power of two.

Part II
Other Readings for Discussion

Black Elk's Vision

As a young child of the Oglala Lakota Sioux, Black Elk had been given a vision; a mighty vision which would lead him on a personal journey intended to result in the peace and flourishing of his people. He was born in December of 1863, the year tribes recorded as, "The Winter when the Four Crows Were Killed." Far to the east America was engaged in the great Civil War. Very little attention was given to happenings in the West.

During his early childhood, Black Elk and the people of the Sioux Nation were free to live their lives as they had for centuries. As a boy he learned to fish, to hunt and use a bow, to ride, and to take part in the celebrations so vital to the life of the tribe. A simple man, Black Elk never learned to read or write, he spoke only Lakota, yet amazingly this one simple man would live to experience more cultural upheaval in his early years than most of us would experience in a lifetime.

Over the course of his life, Black Elk would find himself at the Battle of the Little Big Horn; at Fort Robinson when his cousin, the great leader Crazy Horse, was killed; in exile with Sitting Bull and Gall; and at Wounded Knee during the time of the Ghost Dance movement and the Great Massacre. He was witness to the government's unrelenting efforts to take from the Lakota their sacred Black Hills, and even beyond the land, their very way of life.

With the help of his mighty vision, Black Elk was able to unfold symbols and metaphors in very unique ways so that the lessons learned built on one another and, in the end, laid out before us an ancient path toward inner strength and a balanced life. The challenge is to lift those meanings from one generation into another so that in re-examining them we too may have the direction, a way for us to go.

Name Your Heroes

Knowing we are not alone is a source of comfort as we continue to go through life. Our journey is made much easier knowing that someone else is there, sharing our joys and our sorrows. Sometimes it helps to think of those gone before, who traveled our same path and serve as models for our life.

Joseph Campbell often referred to the hero and the hero path. "A hero," he tells us, "is someone who has found something or done something beyond the normal range of achievement and experience. He has given his life to something bigger than himself." While in your place of solitude and peace, you were asked to draw a circle containing your immediate concerns. Now you are to examine these concerns and determine whether they add to your life or take away from it. Keep in mind, your hoop contains both positive and negative elements: heroes and demons. You begin by placing your issues in some kind of order, always keeping the positive ones close and the negative ones toward the rim, away from the center. You are also asked to name them. Are they your heroes or your demons? "Identification reduces the perceived strength of the negative force and gives you more control over its power. It no longer can feed on your fear. In the same way, those positive forces become more prominent, giving you a strength you never realized you had. No one will ever be totally free from negative forces. There will always be demons invading your hoop."

By repeating this exercise you will begin to become more and more aware of an unconsciousness that lies deep within. Visiting the quietness of your special place, drawing your hoop of containment limiting your concerns, the identification of your heroes and demons, are early steps toward self discovery. Each experience will bring increased inner strength because you are in control of the conflicting forces within each of us. Only through self discovery and meditation do we leave the distractions and worldly demands, and turn our sights inward, unlocking who we really are and what we really can become.

Part III
Other Activities

The following is a list of other activities for your sessions:

1. Bring your favorite "comfort food" to share with your partner.
2. Bring a photo of someone who has had a major impact on your life.
3. Listen to any or all of the songs and discuss the metaphors in the lyrics:

    Elton John "The Bridge"

    Mamas and Papas "Twelve-Thirty"

    Suggest a song that has meaning for you

For more information and activities visit www.pompanobooks.com

About the Author

Linda L. Stampoulos lives in New Jersey, and often travels to the West to research material her books. After completing her Undergraduate and Graduate Degrees at Montclair State University, she went on to Columbia University, to earn her Doctorate in Education. She has taught at both the Undergraduate and Graduate levels in the Schools of Health Foundations and Educational Foundations at Montclair State University. A large portion of her curriculum included the works of Joseph Campbell. In addition, she has devoted over twenty-five years to work in the field of Substance Abuse Prevention and Treatment Services.

Her last book, *Two on a Bridge, The Guidebook* was recently published. The *Workbook* is a companion tool which offers the reader activities to help process the principles outlined in the Guidebook. Her other works include *The Redemption of Black Elk* which was published in English as well as in German, *Black Elks Vermachtnis*. She has also contributed to the Images of America series: *Visiting the Grand Canyon, Views of Early Tourism* which was listed among the Southwest Books of the Year, Best Reading 2004. In addition, she has previously worked on several projects with Native American author Kenny Shields, Jr. to produce: *Fort Peck Indian Reservation*; *The Little Bighorn, Tiospaye*; and *The Grand Canyon: Native People and Early Visitors*. These and other works can be found at Pompanobooks.com

www.ingramcontent.com/pod-product-compliance
Lightning Source LLC
Chambersburg PA
CBHW060823090426
42738CB00002B/86